FAMOUS NATIVE AMERICANS

Sacagawea

By Ann Byers

Cavendish
Square

New York

Published in 2021 by Cavendish Square Publishing, LLC
243 5th Avenue, Suite 136, New York, NY 10016

Copyright © 2021 by Cavendish Square Publishing, LLC

First Edition

Website: cavendishsq.com

This publication represents the opinions and views of the author based on his or her personal experience, knowledge, and research. The information in this book serves as a general guide only. The author and publisher have used their best efforts in preparing this book and disclaim liability rising directly or indirectly from the use and application of this book.

All websites were available and accurate when this book was sent to press.

Library of Congress Cataloging-in-Publication Data

Names: Byers, Ann, author.
Title: Sacagawea / Ann Byers.
Description: First edition. | New York, NY : Cavendish Square Publishing, LLC, 2021. | Series: The Inside Guide: Famous Native Americans | Includes bibliographical references and index.
Identifiers: LCCN 2019042253 (print) | LCCN 2019042254 (ebook) | ISBN 9781502650665 (hardcover) | ISBN 9781502650641 (pbk.) | ISBN 9781502650658 (set) | ISBN 9781502650672 (ebook)
Subjects: LCSH: Sacagawea–Juvenile literature. | Shoshoni Indians–Biography–Juvenile literature. | Shoshoni women–Biography–Juvenile literature. | Lewis and Clark Expedition (1804-1806)–Biography–Juvenile literature.
Classification: LCC F592.7.S12 B94 2021 (print) | LCC F592.7.S12 (ebook) | DDC 978.004/9745740092 [B]–dc23
LC record available at https://lccn.loc.gov/2019042253
LC ebook record available at https://lccn.loc.gov/2019042254

Editor: Kristen Susienka
Copy Editor: Rebecca Rohan
Designer: Deanna Paternostro

The photographs in this book are used by permission and through the courtesy of: Cover, p. 6 Bettmann/Bettmann/Getty Images; p. 4 Smith Collection/Gado/Getty Images; pp. 7, 15 (top), 20, 28 (bottom left) Everett Historical/Shutterstock.com; pp. 9, 13, 29 (left) GraphicaArtis/Getty Images; pp. 10, 16 MPI/Getty Images; p. 12 Ben Wittick/Buyenlarge/Getty Images; p. 14 ZUMA Press, Inc./Alamy Stock Photo; p. 15 (bottom) Katherine Welles/Shutterstock.com; p. 18 Stock Montage/Getty Images; p. 19 © North Wind Picture Archives; p. 22 Danita Delimont/Alamy Stock Photo; p. 24 History and Art Collection/ Alamy Stock Photo; p. 25 Daniel D Malone/Shutterstock.com; p. 26 Manny Ceneta/AFP via Getty Images; p. 27 AF archive/Alamy Stock Photo; p. 28 (top left) Jim Black/Shutterstock.com; p. 28 (top right) Nawrocki/ClassicStock/Getty Images; p. 28 (bottom right) Ace Diamond/ Shutterstock.com; p. 29 (right) Pictures Now/Alamy Stock Photo.

Some of the images in this book illustrate individuals who are models. The depictions do not imply actual situations or events.

CPSIA compliance information: Batch #CS20CSQ: For further information contact Cavendish Square Publishing LLC, New York, New York, at 1-877-980-4450.

Printed in the United States of America

Find us on

CONTENTS

Sacagawea was part of the Shoshone tribe. This image imagines what a Shoshone village looked like.

HEROES OF THE UNITED STATES

All over the world, groups have stories of men and women who have done great things for their countries. These people are part of a country's legends or history. The United States has such stories too. Some legends and stories of historical figures are known to all people in the United States. Other stories of brave men and women are unique to different groups of people who call this country home.

Native American communities in the United States have different cultures, or groups with similar backgrounds and ways of life, with many stories detailing heroic men and women. Tribes such as the Apache, Navajo, Sioux, and Shoshone each have their own celebrated figures. You may have heard of some of these people before, such as Pocahontas or Geronimo. Others might be new, like Sequoyah or Crazy Horse. All of them helped their communities and earned a place in the history of the United States.

Sacagawea

One of the most well-known Native American women of the past was Sacagawea. She lived in the 1800s, during a time when America was young and eager to grow. Ideas of America stretching from "sea to shining sea," or **Manifest Destiny**, were just beginning to form in the minds of

some of the country's leaders. President Thomas Jefferson had gained new land through the **Louisiana Purchase** of 1803, adding to this mindset. A period of exploration, discovery, and adventure took hold of America.

President Jefferson wanted people to explore the new land of the Louisiana Purchase. He asked Meriwether Lewis and William Clark to go out and document what they saw. Others who went with them on the journey formed what's known today as the Corps of Discovery.

Sacagawea was an important part of Lewis and Clark's journey to the West.

This illustration of Lewis and Clark, with Sacagawea and her husband in the background, is from 1906, 100 years after the journey ended.

Sacagawea was a young woman when she met the two explorers. They would change her life. Lewis and Clark asked her and her husband to help them on their journey. They traveled through unknown

THE LOUISIANA PURCHASE

In 1803, President Thomas Jefferson completed a deal to purchase over 828,000 square miles (2,144,510 square kilometers) of land from France. The European country had owned the land for decades, trading with the native people there. A series of conflicts and treaties led to the French emperor, Napoleon Bonaparte, selling the Louisiana Territory to Jefferson. This acquisition meant the United States now owned nearly double the land the country had previously. America was now the owner of territory east and west of the Mississippi River. The deal was also completed cheaply— nearly three cents for every acre (0.4 hectares). This deal meant the United States was on its way to becoming a powerful and vast young country. Overall, the Louisiana Purchase led to westward expansion—the move from primarily dense, East Coast areas to the unknown wildernesses of the West. Over the next century, many would make the journey from one part of the country to the other, in search of adventure, gold, or new opportunities.

Fast Fact

The Lewis and Clark Expedition traveled from Saint Louis, Missouri, to the Pacific Ocean in what is now Oregon.

parts, meeting people they didn't know and encountering animals that might seek to harm them. It would be an exciting but dangerous mission. When she said yes to their offer, Sacagawea started the trip of her life.

This map shows how one artist interpreted the Louisiana Purchase. It was much more than President Thomas Jefferson had expected.

She acted as an interpreter and at times a guide through wild **terrain** and Native American lands, helping the men complete the mission President Thomas Jefferson had given them.

Sacagawea's life wasn't easy, but it was full of new discoveries, bold journeys, and bravery. Above all, it helped prove women were capable of tremendous accomplishments. They wouldn't let the possibility of danger get in their way. Let's learn more about Sacagawea and how she became so famous today.

This painting shows a scene described in Clark's journal. The group met members of the Chinook tribe on the Columbia River. Sacagawea spoke to them.

Chapter Two

A GUIDE AND HELPER

Little is known about Sacagawea's early life. Stories say she was born into the Lemhi Shoshone tribe around 1788. Her tribe lived in the Salmon River region of what's now the state of Idaho. The Rocky Mountains surrounded Sacagawea and her people. They had lived there ever since other tribes had pushed the Shoshone off the flat land they once called home. They became mountain dwellers but did come down occasionally to hunt bison on the Great Plains. They used the bison for food, clothing, and other supplies.

Captured!

Neighboring tribes included a group called the Hidatsa. The Hidatsa tribe hunted bison too. They had guns and used them to hunt. They also were known to capture people from other tribes.

Sometimes they sold the people to white men—the strangers who came to their land to trade and hunt.

One day in 1800, the Shoshone were

Fast Fact

"Sacagawea" has two meanings, depending on the language. In Shoshone, it means "boat pusher." In Hidatsa, it means "bird woman."

THE SHOSHONE TRIBE

In ancient times, the Shoshone were hunters and gatherers. They hunted animals and gathered roots and berries to eat. They also fished in rivers. The men hunted, and the women cooked and took care of their homes. Sacagawea also gathered food to eat and used her skills on her journey with Lewis and Clark.

In 1800, there were three Shoshone groups. The Western Shoshone built cone-shaped houses from grasses. The Eastern and Northern groups lived in tepees covered with bison skins. The groups were divided into smaller groups called "bands." Sacagawea belonged to the Lemhi band of the Northern Shoshone.

Each Shoshone band lived by itself; however, all the Northern bands came together twice a year. They went to the Great Plains to hunt bison. Today, about 41,000 Shoshone descendants live throughout the United States.

In 1900, when this picture was taken, many Northern Shoshone still lived in tents called tepees covered with bison skins.

hunting on the flat land. Twelve-year-old Sacagawea was there. When she least expected it, someone from the Hidatsa tribe caught her! They took her to their village and eventually sold her to a Frenchman named Toussaint Charbonneau, who traded animal furs with and lived among the Hidatsa. Sacagawea became his wife. Together, they lived in a village with the Hidatsa and an **affiliated** tribe called the Mandan.

A Long Trip

In 1804, two white men came to the area where Sacagawea and Charbonneau lived. They were Meriwether Lewis and William Clark, men sent by President Thomas Jefferson to explore new land the United States had acquired from France. Sacagawea and Charbonneau were curious about the newcomers and traveled to meet them at another Mandan village where they'd stopped for the winter.

Speaking with Charbonneau, Lewis and Clark discovered Sacagawea could talk with members of the Shoshone

Meriwether Lewis (*left*) and William Clark (*right*) were co-leaders of the journey through the Louisiana Territory.

tribes they'd likely meet on the way. This was useful because it was unknown how the Native American groups would treat the newcomers. Lewis and Clark hired Charbonneau and Sacagawea as translators, although Sacagawea was not paid for her help.

Traveling

A few months before the group was ready to start their journey, Sacagawea gave birth to a baby boy. His name was Jean Baptiste, and he would be the smallest and youngest member of the group. Sacagawea traveled with him strapped to her back.

Besides being a translator, Sacagawea helped the group navigate around some of the mountains. She also found roots and berries for everyone to eat.

Altogether, the journey took them from the Mandan village in North Dakota all the way to the Pacific Ocean. It took seven months to get there, starting in April 1805.

Sacagawea carried her son, Jean Baptiste, on her back for much of the journey.

On the Trail

Many of the Native Americans the group met had never seen white people before. At first, some of the Native Americans thought the group might attack them. However, when they saw Sacagawea with her baby, they believed the white people had come in peace.

One of the Native American groups Lewis and Clark met was the Shoshone, the tribe Sacagawea had been born into and been taken from. There, Sacagawea had a surprise. Her brother was the chief! They had a happy **reunion**. After the meeting, he sold Lewis and Clark horses so they could get across the Rocky Mountains.

William Clark

On the journey, Sacagawea became good friends with William Clark. He took care of her when she got sick, and he helped protect her and her baby during a dangerous flood. Clark wrote about Sacagawea in his journal that documented the expedition. He called her "the Indian [Native] woman" and "Sah-kah-gar we a." In 1812, after Sacagawea's death, Clark became the guardian of Sacagawea's children, Jean Baptiste and her daughter Lizette.

The trip ended in 1806. Sacagawea's husband went back to trading furs, taking Sacagawea and young Jean Baptiste with him. Not much is known about her life after that. However, it's believed that she gave birth to Lizette in 1812. Many stories state that a few months later, Sacagawea got sick and died. She was 25 years old.

Before joining the journey, William Clark served in the US army. He fought battles, made maps, and worked as a spy.

Fast Fact

Jean Baptiste's nickname was Pompey. William Clark carved his own name into a rock formation he named Pompey's Pillar, near the Yellowstone River. It's now a national **monument**.

On the return trip, Clark carved this into a sandstone rock he named Pompey's Pillar.

After the Lewis and Clark Expedition, wagon trains streamed west as thousands of people began to settle the new territory.

Chapter Three

THE EXPEDITION

During the time that Lewis and Clark traveled with Sacagawea, Thomas Jefferson was president. He dreamed of finding a water passage that would cut through America and connect the Atlantic and Pacific Oceans. This fabled river was called the Northwest Passage. It had been a rumor for some time, and Jefferson now wanted to find out if it was real. People had been searching for this passage for many years. Each quest affected the Native American groups living in the territories near where the passage was thought to be, and Lewis and Clark's expedition was no different. Native groups like Sacagawea's had lived in these areas for centuries, and Lewis and Clark's appearance would change their lives.

Other Goals of the Trip

Jefferson wasn't just concerned about the Northwest Passage. He also wanted to know all about the Louisiana Territory. What plants were there? Were there any new kinds of animals? What was the weather like? He'd also hoped to set up trading networks with the Native American people, in the hope that relations between the Native Americans and settlers would be peaceful when more people moved onto Native American lands.

He chose Meriwether Lewis to lead what would be one of the most detailed and longest trips of exploration in the country. Lewis was friends

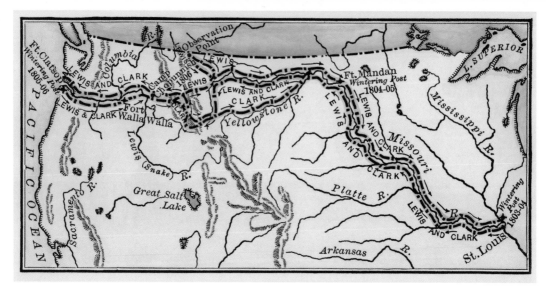

This map shows the routes there and back that the Corps of Discovery took through the West.

with William Clark, who had served with him at a military training camp. Together—and with the help of Sacagawea—they would make history.

Getting Ready

Lewis and Clark were asked to document everything they encountered. Before leaving, Lewis got special training in mapmaking, **surveying**, botany, mathematics, fossils, anatomy, and medicine. He and Clark were leaders of the group of explorers that would eventually total about 45 people, including Sacagawea. It was their responsibility to ensure as many lived through the journey as possible.

Trouble on the Trail

Members of the Corps of Discovery, including Sacagawea, were instructed to greet any Native American communities as nicely as possible. Lewis had purchased gifts to give

Fast Fact

Lewis's Newfoundland dog, Seaman, came along on the trip. He helped hunt and guard.

EXPEDITION JOURNALS

William Clark, Meriwether Lewis, and several other members of the Corps of Discovery kept detailed journals during the expedition. Every day, or every few days, they would write about their experiences on the journey. In total, the diary writers would write over 140,000 words, spanning from March 1804 to September 1806. Sometimes these entries described the day's events; other times they mentioned new animals or plants the group encountered, geographical features, or the weather. Today, these journals are valuable primary sources that tell the story of one of the most successful and peaceful journeys across the United States in its early history.

William Clark kept detailed notes of the wildlife and plants they met along the way. This is one example from his journals.

to the Native Americans they met, since gift-giving was a sign of friendship. This was one of the reasons Sacagawea was so important to the journey. She could speak to some native communities. She and Jean Baptiste also signaled to native groups that the white men weren't dangerous. Along the way, most Native Americans treated the group well, especially the Nez Perce. However, not everyone was kind to them.

One incident happened when the group was on the way back from the Pacific Ocean, where their outward journey ended. Lewis and Clark had taken separate routes. Lewis's group, which didn't include Sacagawea, faced the Blackfeet. Members of this Native American group attacked Lewis and his men. Two of the Native Americans were killed in fighting. However, none of the Corps members were hurt. In fact, only one person died on the entire journey.

Lewis and Clark gave this Jefferson Peace Medal to the native leaders they met as a sign of peace.

Fast Fact

The group recorded 120 animal specimens and 200 plant samples on their expedition to the Pacific Ocean.

Other dangers concerned wildlife or illness. Sacagawea was thought to have become ill from bacteria that was on grizzly bear meat she ate. Weather could also affect the group. Storms, floods, hail, and heat took their toll.

Returning

After the trip ended, Lewis, Clark, Sacagawea, and the rest of the Corps of Discovery were heroes. They arrived back in the Mandan village in the summer of 1806. Once Sacagawea and her husband left the group, Lewis and Clark continued to Saint Louis, where their journey officially ended. Altogether, the Corps traveled 8,000 miles (12,874 km) on foot, on horseback, or by boat.

Not much is known about what happened to Sacagawea after she returned from the journey. Perhaps the Mandan were curious about what she'd seen. For her help, she received no payment. Her husband, however, was paid. It's clear she and Clark kept in touch. He eventually took care of Sacagawea's two children.

As the years turned to decades, new settlers arrived. They used the Corps's records of the area to navigate. They met Native American groups, perhaps some that Sacagawea had spoken to. However, over time, relations between Native Americans and settlers became strained. Eventually, many Native Americans were sent to reservations away from their home. By 1890, most of the Native Americans in the West lived on reservations. Sacagawea's Shoshone band went to the Fort Hall reservation in Idaho.

In the late 1800s and 1900s, more settlers moved to the West. Manifest Destiny had become a reality.

Some people might think Sacagawea's help in the Corps led to the end of many Native Americans' ways of life. However, others think of Sacagawea as a woman who helped a new America form.

This statue of Sacagawea and her son stands in the Lemhi River Valley in Idaho, where Sacagawea was born.

Chapter Four

A MODERN HERO

Almost 100 years after her famous trip, Sacagawea's name was little more than a **footnote** in history books. No one knew much about her or her role in Lewis and Clark's trip. However, that changed in 1902, when a woman named Eva Dye wrote a book about the Lewis and Clark Expedition. Unlike other accounts of the journey, she made Sacagawea the hero of the story. Many people read the book and learned about Sacagawea then. Ever since, Sacagawea has been a hero for the whole country.

Hero for Native Americans

Native Americans can point to Sacagawea to show that they were very important in America's history. Her bravery, strength, and ability to bridge the sometimes wide gap between Native American and white settlers changed the United States. She helped Native Americans and white settlers work together and learn more about each other.

Hero for Women

Sacagawea is a **role model** for women. She was the only female on a dangerous trip with lots of men. Lewis wrote that she was as strong and

Eva Dye wrote five books about the American West, including Sacagawea's story.

dependable as the men. She was also a good mother. She's an example for women who want to do new and challenging things in their lives.

Hero for Young People

Sacagawea was a teenager when she started with the expedition. Even though she was young, she worked hard and did her job. In fact, she did more than she had to. Grown men respected her and relied on her for help and guidance. She showed that young people can do great things.

Fast Fact

Sacagawea's wish was to see the Pacific Ocean. She got her wish when she joined Clark and some other men on a fishing trip.

Telling Her Story

Sacagawea lives on in popular culture today. Many books have been written about her. Many videos have been made showing her life. People

GOLDEN DOLLAR

In 2000, a new one-dollar coin was made. The image on the front of the coin is Sacagawea carrying Jean Baptiste on her back. It's called the Golden Dollar. The coin is made of copper and brass, but it looks like gold. The artist found a young Shoshone woman to use as a model.

The back of the coin shows an eagle and 17 stars. The United States had 17 states at the time of the Lewis and Clark Expedition. Now, the Golden Dollars have different pictures on the back. The artist who drew the picture of Sacagawea was paid 5,000 Golden Dollars for her drawing. It's one of many **depictions** of the Shoshone **icon** known to exist today, and the coin continues to be seen as a symbol highlighting the importance of Native American people.

This Golden Dollar coin is from 2007. Every year since 2009, a new Sacagawea coin is issued with a new picture on the back.

A Shoshone woman (*left*) and a Hidatsa woman (*right*) accept a plaque from President Bill Clinton in 2001. The plaque honors Sacagawea with the official title of Honorary Sergeant, Regular Army.

have written plays that tell her story. Some of the plays are made for schoolchildren to put on. There's even a musical version of her story, called *Sacagawea*.

Fast Fact

In 2001, US President Bill Clinton gave Sacagawea the title of Honorary Sergeant in the Army. She carried out the duties of an official army officer.

Sacagawea is remembered in movies today. The 2006 movie *Night at the Museum* cast Mizuo Peck in the role of Sacagawea and Robin Williams in the role of Theodore Roosevelt.

Sacagawea is also in the *Night at the Museum* movies. These movies aren't true stories, but they show how famous a figure she is. In the movies, she's an important character. She guides people and is brave.

Sacagawea is one of America's most popular heroes. Rivers and mountains have been named after her. There are many monuments to her across the country. The US Navy named a ship the *Sacagawea*. A crater on the planet Venus is even named for her! Sacagawea's life story shows that people can use their unique strengths and skills to do great things.

THINK ABOUT IT!

Use these questions to help you think more deeply about this topic.

1. What do you think it was like when Sacagawea was kidnapped?

2. Why did Lewis and Clark want Sacagawea's help on their journey?

3. Why did Thomas Jefferson call for the Lewis and Clark Expedition?

4. Why do you think Sacagawea wasn't paid for her help?

5. What are some ways Sacagawea is remembered today?

TIMELINE

Sacagawea's Life	World Events

1788
Sacagawea is born in what's now Idaho.

1800
Sacagawea is captured by the Hidatsa.

1803
The United States buys the Louisiana Territory from France.

1804–1806
The Lewis and Clark Expedition explores the new territory.

1805
Sacagawea gives birth to a boy and joins the Lewis and Clark Expedition.

1812
Sacagawea gives birth to a girl; four months later, she dies.

1813
William Clark adopts Sacagawea's two children.

1890
The US government announces that the West has been settled.

GLOSSARY

affiliate: To be connected to.

depiction: A representation of someone.

footnote: A minor character or fact.

icon: Someone held in high regard who stands for something.

Louisiana Purchase: The United States' buying of the Louisiana Territory from France in 1803.

Manifest Destiny: The idea that the United States should expand from one coast to the other because it was its God-given right.

monument: A statue or building that honors someone for their achievements.

reunion: A meeting of people who have been apart for a while.

role model: An example of what someone should be like.

surveying: Determining a piece of land's characteristics, such as its size, shape, and boundaries.

terrain: Ground.

FIND OUT MORE

Books

Jazynka, Kitson. *Sacagawea*. Washington, DC: National Geographic, 2015.

Meltzer, Brad. *I Am Sacagawea*. New York, NY: Dial Books, 2017.

Websites

National Geographic: Lewis and Clark Expedition

kids.nationalgeographic.com/explore/history/lewis-and-clark/
This illustrated website guides young visitors through the Lewis and Clark Expedition.

Scholastic: Lewis and Clark

teacher.scholastic.com/activities/lewis_clark/prepare.htm
This website outlines the Lewis and Clark Expedition in a fun and creative way.

Shoshone Facts for Kids

www.bigorrin.org/shoshone_kids.htm
This site describes Shoshone culture and life both today and in the past. It has many links to more information.

INDEX